GROUP GLUE

The connective power of how simple
questions lead to great conversations

BY

JEFFREY T. COOK

REDINALS PUBLISHING LLC

Visit our website at www.GroupGlueBook.com.

Cover Design by Alessandro Migliorato

Cover image used under license from Shutterstock.com

eBook ISBN: 978-0-9981266-0-9

Print ISBN: 978-0-9981266-1-6

DEDICATION

First and foremost, this book is dedicated to my first "group" where I experimented my questions daily...loved our "Traction" meetings!

I could not publish this without a formal dedication to my wife Teresa and our three boys (Tyler, Braden, Carson)...thank you for putting up with all of my questions!

TABLE OF CONTENTS

CHAPTER ONE – INTRODUCTION

PART I: The birth of the first question

It started in a meeting.

That's the answer to the number one question I get as to why I was writing a book about questions. Back in late 2005, I took a new job as manager of a technical support team located in Alpharetta, Georgia. For a guy who lived his entire life in Illinois, moving South was a bit of a culture shock. From grits, fried okra, and boiled peanuts—this was a far cry from the suburbs of Chicago. Good news is that 75 percent of my new team had just relocated from the middle of Kansas, so we were all transplants. My job was to motivate a team of very seasoned staff with an average tenure of 15 years. How do you motivate such a mature, seasoned team to change what they have been doing the same way over the past 15 years? As an avid reader, I found inspiration from a book called "The Goal." In that book, a single sentence would be the catalyst for how I would lead this team. That quote was this: "Tell me how you will measure me, and I will tell you how I will behave." Such a brilliant leadership idea, but how did this lead to me writing over 1000 questions and be persuaded to write a book about it?

That quote inspired me to not only measure this team (which almost all leaders do with their own team), but I wanted to talk about the simple measurements that we should watch every single day. I only had four measurements we would review daily as a team so as not to overwhelm our meetings with typical "management speak." These daily meetings would be called numerous things over the years:

- Stand-Ups (because no one could sit down to keep them short)

- Daily briefings

- Traction Meetings (get "traction" each morning)

- Just Plain Crazy Meetings (because meeting every day is crazy)

For my new seasoned team, this was the genesis of my questions.

It wasn't a popular choice, but I was going to meet with the team each morning for 15 minutes to discuss what we did yesterday, what we need to look out for today and then start bonding the team together. They all complained and thought it was a waste of time, but since I was new, they gave me a little slack. So during one of the first few meetings after discussing our previous day, the measurements we want to strive for, and a quick person-by-person around the room asking for any other issues—I popped this question at them:

What kind of things do you hate spending money on?

To be honest, I'm not really sure why I asked THAT question first. Could have been a recent bad experience with a car repair, home repair, or medical bills, but regardless of my WHY, I noticed an ENERGY that came to the room once people started to answer the question. People wanted to participate. People wanted to share. People were interested in what their peers had to say. Many had a shared experience. Many had a sympathetic and compassionate response. The simpler the question, the more they would talk. And the talking did not stop in our meeting. It continued all day. And then the stories behind the answers continued. Yes, we were still productive, but we also learned a little bit more about how a teammate thinks, feels, acts and overcomes. So I kept asking the questions.

To be transparent, I didn't want to come up with a question each day, but my team really enjoyed them. Being new to the team, I really enjoyed getting to know these folks too. Fast-forward to today and I have collected over 1000 questions that I have asked my teams in the past 11 years. Do they ever get sick of the questions? Not yet. And as a teammate moves up in the organization and new ones arrive, the questions help the new employees adapt and grow to this existing team.

When speaking about my questions, I'll get the occasional manager or director who questions if this would work for his or her team with employees spread out all over the world. They can see value for those people in a room but what about employees that work from afar? Does it still work? I can attest that the questions work even better for those remote. At least 10 percent and then over 40 percent of my team have been working out of the office all over the country, and they would say that these meetings...these questions...bring them closer to their peers more than any other time in their employment. "It's like I was right there in the office." Those were their words and not mine. This meeting and the connection shared while we experienced each answer kept them close. How many times do you gather up all of your remote employees? I would guess it's not daily.

PART II: Trying Questions on a New Audience

Maybe I got lucky in that one company because we were all transplants, and the questions kept us a tight knit group. So I tried a new experiment as I took on a new role at a new company.

This new company was vastly different from my old company—I went from a very structured, corporate environment (cubes, casual Fridays, and pre-meetings) to an "open concept" floor plan where everyone (including the CTO) just has a desk with no walls...just a desk, plus a game room, a kegerator, full bar, Nerf guns, and bean bags. Our desks were these super cool desks with a motor that moves it up and down so you can stand or sit when working, but you get the idea. Here I am, a brand new employee with over a 150 new coworkers. How did I get to rapidly know them and, in turn, they got to know a little bit about me? Questions. I had a 4ft x 6ft whiteboard leaning up against a wall with the title "Question of the Day" and I added a simple question each day. Guess what happened?

It started with a few brave souls verbally answering the question as they walked by to fill up their coffee mugs. Then a few more would stop by and give their answer and ask me mine. Soon it evolved into people wanting to share their answer with everyone, so they got down on their hands and knees to write their answer on the whiteboard that was leaning against the wall.

Here is a snapshot of the whiteboard question board. The question was, "What was your favorite TV Show growing up?"

I soon had daily visits from people all over the building. Another group was inspired to have their own Question of the Day. I had people say they love the question each morning as much as their cup of coffee. I had people asking for the new question when I walked in the door or when I was a little slow in writing the new question on the board. Even the CEO started to participate as he walked by the area. It was contagious, it was simple, and it broke down the walls of a brand new, introverted employee in a matter of weeks.

It's been two years since I started this job and the "Question of the Day" continues. The only difference now? I have a new whiteboard on a stand with wheels so people can answer the question standing up.

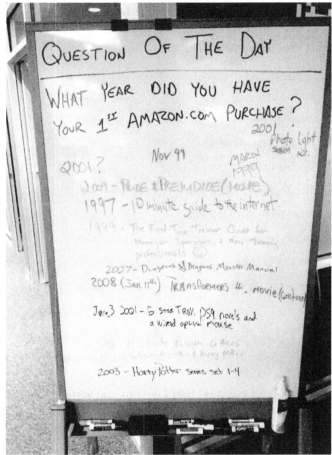

Here is snapshot of the new question board on wheels! The question was, "What year did you have your first Amazon.com purchase?"

Think this is only for a business setting? Try these same

questions in any group setting:

- Book clubs
- Bible studies
- Neighborhood party
- Double date
- The dreaded middle seat on an airplane
- Short term missions trip
- Family reunions
- Holiday parties
- Dinner chats with your kids

How about a scenario like this: I was meeting a coworker from

another part of our business that I did not know at all. I was

meeting her at the airport and then we were hopping in a car

for over six-plus hours of driving to our final destination. Now

you can only talk work for so long, so I started asking some of

these questions. We had an amazing time diving into some

obscure topics, and the time flew by. At the end of the trip, she confessed that she was dreading this trip about as much as I was, but after the questions she really enjoyed the trip because of our conversations started by questions.

Don't believe me yet? Have some anxiety about not wanting to waste time in a meeting or feel weird popping a question on your coworkers? Then ask the question BEFORE your meeting starts with those arriving early. Watch and listen to how they react and what they say. There will be a "buzz" started in the meeting before a single PowerPoint slide is displayed. Do that a few times and more people may start coming to your meetings on time (or even early)!

What I have found is that many teams just don't spend any time getting to know each other. I'm not talking about knowing their deep dark secrets or becoming BFF's (Best Friends Forever), but questions can help you UNDERSTAND that person. Do you see that with your team or individuals on your team? Ever wonder WHY that one guy always reacts a certain way or that lady from sales will constantly talk about certain topics? That person has a long history before meeting you, and the world has shaped them into who they are today. You may be surprised when you experience an answer to a question that gives you that "Ahhh, so that's why they react that way."

Questions can and will lead to a better understanding, and even better, a positive relationship. Open questions will reveal a treasure trove of information that you get to experience. In the end, relationships that you cherish are based on great conversations. Even if you feel these questions are just mediocre, they start the conversation.

To paraphrase a famous Nike marketing program—Just ASK it.

CHAPTER TWO – WELCOME TO GLUE

GLUE – a substance used to stick things tightly together; something that binds together

What do you think of when I say the word GLUE? For me, the first thought goes back to the classic white, rectangular bottle with the orange cap and a gob of hard glue stuck on the top. I have thoughts of gluing paper, cotton balls, and those weird eyeballs with the plastic pupil, rocks, glitter, and yarn. I remember that white, dripping substance was all over my pants, the floor, caked on my hands, and eventually on the two pieces of construction paper used for a first grade art project. Others may remember the glue in the form of white paste that your friend had an appetite to eat when the teacher was not looking.

If you are more of the handyman type, the yellow wood glue

may have been your first thought as it takes you back to the

handmade dresser you build from scrap wood in your garage or

that yellow wood glue is the bonding agent holding your

perfectly mitered edges on that top drawer. If you happen to be

one that has broken anything of value, you may have thought

about that clear glue in a little bottle—about the size of a chap

stick bottle—that saved your neck in high school after you broke

and repaired your mother's family heirloom vase. All of these

glue examples have one thing in common—they all created a

bond.

While you may not think of glue as something that can bring

people together (try super-gluing two siblings together!), it's a

great metaphor to use when talking about how a group of

people can become closer using questions. Questions, like glue, are a binding agent. Ask a group of women about their husbands' worst habits and they immediately form a bond. Ask a group of men about their favorite college football team and the two University of Auburn fans will immediately yell "War Eagle"...and a common bond is created.

Because all questions are not alike or as deep, I have created three levels of questions to help you in your journey to tighten or start the bonding of your team. Keeping with the Glue theme, we have the questions broken down into three areas:

WHITE GLUE questions – get the conversations flowing

YELLOW GLUE questions – getting to the real you

CLEAR GLUE questions – transparent and deep

WHITE GLUE questions—basic and not too deep. Great to start here and get the conversations flowing. As in the color of white glue, everyone starts off as a blank, white sheet of paper.

YELLOW GLUE questions—yellow glue represents the strains of life. A little bit deeper about who we are. It's the faded white version of our true self. These questions go a little bit deeper, but not the gut-wrenching or tear dropping questions that make a room go silent.

TRANSPARENT GLUE questions—once you get past the surface and go deep, transparency is evident. Answering these levels of questions require transparency and boldness to ask and then receive the answer. In a majority of groups, these questions are almost considered taboo. There are very few of these in this book, but if you ask them, be prepared for a deep answer.

To make this book easier to navigate, I have broken the questions up by categories. I took some liberties to get questions to fit into certain categories, but this should help you narrow down a particular set of questions you might want to ask a group. Each category will have the three Glue levels of questions…White, Yellow, Transparent to help you gauge what level is appropriate for your group.

Last, but not least, is the Appendix, where I have narrowed down my top 11 questions I have used. Out of the 1100+ questions to choose, it was a painful task to come up with my top 11, but I can assure you that these questions have created the BEST conversations in that group setting and continued for days/weeks later.

CHAPTER THREE – HOW TO USE THIS BOOK

Still don't get how to use the Group Glue book? Here are a few examples where the questions may bring a quiet, reserved group into a vibrantly, alive team:

IN THE BUSINESS WORLD

- Existing Team—have a team that seems to be in rut?? Or you need to infuse a little life into them again? Start by asking one question a day in an email to your team. Better yet, post it to your internal "collaboration" site that you never seem to use.

- New Team is Forming—great way to kick off or end a meeting of a new team or group that will be working together over a long period of time. Start off with a few of these questions and watch the new connections

form.

- A Very Seasoned Team—a group that has been doing

  something for a long time can "sometimes" become

  routine...maybe even lethargic...use these questions to

  shake up a daily standing meeting.

- That 3-5 minutes before a meeting starts—break the

  awkward silence before a meeting begins with a simple

  question....especially if you're leading the meeting. This

  is a great way to prime the conversation pump and get

  the energy going in the room.

- Traveling with a coworker—ever stuck in a car with a

  coworker as you drive to a customer site? If you got

  hours of road time, this is a lifesaver for an introvert!

Grab the book, pull it out and ask, "Have you seen this interesting new book?"

SMALL BUSINESS OWNER

- Grab a small white board and put it up in your break room. This will generate communication between departments that normally do not communicate much. Your quiet accountant and your best salesperson may have more in common than you think.

- How about at a doctor's office? That question can start in your break room and end up as a question you pose to patents as you examine her newly broken finger.

AT A CONFERENCE

- Round Table Intro—you know the conference...where they sit you in a circle with seven other people from all over the country/world? You might have a blank paper tent to put your name. Drop a question here, and you just might make a new friend that conference.

- Running the Show—Whether you are putting on the conference or just the speaker for the session, questions are a great way to break the ice with your audience. Ask a question to the nearest audience member or group before you begin to talk. Talk about connecting with your audience!

- Extrovert—This is easy for you...ask a unique question beyond your standard "name and company" questions that get asked by everyone else. Don't you want to stand out?

- Lunches—you remember those, don't you? Everyone gets assigned seats so you can mingle with those you do not know. If you are organizing the meal, put the book (or a list of questions) on the table. If you are just a participant, have a handful of these questions to avoid the awkward silence.

DINNER PARTIES

- Nothing starts the party better than questions. As the first few people arrive, throw out a question that will start a conversation that all of the latecomers will be missing out on.

- Is the party dying down? Turn to a chapter and ask the question to the group. The right question can bring the energy back quickly.

NEIGHBORHOOD POOL

- Getting to the pool late? You see one lounge chair next to a complete stranger. Grab that chair, get your suntan lotion on, and pull out this book. The door is now open to talk about this book and ask a question.

SCHOOL

- You should be studying, so put this book away until you leave the library.

BIBLE STUDY

- Before diving into a deep study of Powerful Prayers or discussing the 12 Love Languages, open the group with 2-3 questions. This is a great way to transition from the busy world to a deep discussion.

CHAPTER FOUR – THE BEST QUESTION...PERIOD.

This will be the shortest chapter in the book, but trust me, this one question will be so powerful that you will use it in many areas of your life. I've used this question at the dinner table for years with my own kids and with adults, and they will all say that it is powerful, emotional, deep and engaging. Try it for one week with your kids and you will be surprised by what they answer and even more surprised by how they respond to YOUR answers.

I will also add this—during a missions trip to Macedonia to work in an orphanage, this question (and the shared answers) was the highlight of the trip. It can be used <u>anywhere</u>.

Here is the magic question:

What was your high and what was your low of the day?

That's it. Shocker, huh? Don't believe me? Just try it. Turn to the nearest person and ask that question. You may get a weird look, but the answers will come. You may even learn something from your son, daughter, spouse, coworker, or the guy sitting next you on your flight back to Des Moines.

CHAPTER FIVE – GROWING UP QUESTIONS

The questions in chapter were designed to get to know you, the family you grew up in, and the history of your life journey. There is an incredible about of information you can learn about someone by hearing how they got from birth all the way to now. There is a reason I put this chapter early in the book— everyone has a story before they met you. Use these questions to find out that story, and I'm sure you will uncover a lot of your group saying "me to" with many of these answers.

White Glue Questions (Growing Up)

1.   What is your earliest childhood memory?

2.   Name your favorite children's story.

3.   What is your favorite cartoon character and why?

4.   How did you learn to ride a bicycle?

5.   What was your favorite thing to play with as a child?

6.   What was your favorite childhood toy?

7.   What was the first car you drove?

8.   What was the first car you owned?

9.   What does the bedroom where you "grew-up" look like now?

10. As a teenager, what was hanging on the walls in your bedroom?

11. What was the worst whoop'n or punishment your parents ever gave you?

AS A TEENAGER, WHAT WAS HANGING ON THE WALLS IN YOUR BEDROOM?

"One of my walls was completely covered with Matt Dillon, C.Thomas Howell & Sylvester Stallone. Another wall had artwork that my sister and I did, and tapestries of Led Zeppelin & The Who. Another had a crucifix, and gymnastics medals & ribbons we both had won. The last little wall was covered in pictures of models from fashion magazine's. All walls were covered, mostly from my sister Mary." - *TRACY P.*

---

12. What was your worst summer or part-time job?

13. Describe your best or worst experience at summer camp.

14. What is a fashion trend that you wore (in the 70s, 80s, etc.) that you would now be embarrassed to wear?

15. Where did you live at age five?

16. What was one of the most fun things you and your college roommate did together?

17. When you were six years old, what did you want to be when you grew up?

18. What was your favorite age and why?

19. What's the worst trouble you got into when you were young?

20. What one adult rule did you always disagree with?

21. What was your favorite game when you were a kid?

22. What do you miss most about childhood?

23. What was your nickname growing up and do people still call you that?

24. What clubs were you a member of in high school and are you still interested in any of them?

25. Can you recall any "snow days" where school was cancelled in your youth?

26. What's the one place you need to visit when you go to your "hometown" or place of birth?

27. What was (or needs to be) the thing you want to show your children when you visit your hometown or place of birth?

28. Is your hometown in better or worse shape since you left?

29. What famous line did your parents use over and over?

30. Which of your parents' rules do you really appreciate now and why?

31. Did you ever run away from home and for how long?

32. What is the funniest story your mother tells about you?

33. What do you miss most about being a kid?

34. Where did you grow up?

35. What did you collect or have a collection of as a child?

36. What was the most mischievous thing you did as a child?

37. What's the funniest thing you did as a kid that your parents still talk about to this day?

38. Have you ever gone back to the town where you grew up in and if so, how has it changed?

39. What fad did you pick up that you are most embarrassed about?

40. What is the one thing you always wanted as a kid but never got?

41. What age were you when you had your most embarrassing hairstyle?

42. What one object in your hometown are you most embarrassed about?

43. Knowing what you know now, what ONE thing would you change about your high school career?

44. Generally speaking, what type of kid were you (eg: spoiled, rebellious, well-behaved, quiet, obnoxious, etc.)?

45. What was your favorite meal growing up?

46. What did you like best about your hometown?

47. Name one poster or picture you had on your walls as a teenager?

48. How many siblings do you have and where do you fall in the birth order?

49. Who in your family always looks different each year at your family celebrations?

50. Do you remember shopping for school supplies and what one specific item do you remember getting that was unique?

51. What was your first pet?

52. Name all the type/breed of dogs you have owned over the years.

Yellow Glue Questions (Growing Up)

1. What is your favorite tradition from your youth?

2. What is your favorite memory with someone other than family?

3. What do you consider to be the most valuable thing you owned as a child, teenager, and young adult?

4. Have you ever walked in on your parents doing something embarrassing?

5. Which member of your family has had the greatest influence on your current way of thinking?

6. How many children do you want and what is the breakdown between girls and boys?

7. What is the biggest mistake you have made with raising your kids?

8. Have you experienced positive or negative situations involving a family business?

9. What is your favorite advice from your father?

10. What is the best way to love your kids?

11. What is your favorite advice from your mother?

12. What is your favorite advice from a sibling?

13. What is your favorite advice from a grandparent?

14. What is the best way to love your parents?

15. Outside of your immediate family (spouse, kids, parents, siblings), who is your favorite living relative?

16. Outside of your immediate family (spouse, kids, parents, siblings), who is your favorite non-living relative?

17. What did you do today (or this week, this month) to bring your family closer?

18. What town do you consider your "hometown" and why did your parent(s) settle there?

19. If you could have been told one thing that you weren't told when you were a teenager, what would you like to have heard?

20. When you were in grade school, what did you want to be when you grew up and why?

21. Who was your hero when you were a child, and what did you do to be like them?

22. What "group" did you belong to in high school?

23. Share the biggest argument you had with your parents.

24. If I asked your high school friends what they thought you would be doing today, what would they say?

25. If you could choose any couple, besides your parents, to adopt you at birth, who would they be?

26. What was your favorite year in school and why?

27. When you look back on pictures of yourself, what age are you most embarrassed about?

28. Name the one neighbor you did not get along with when you were growing up?

29. Who in your extended family do you live the closest to (distance)?

30. Who in your extended family are you relationally the closest?

Transparent Glue Questions (Growing Up)

1. Are there any relatives or siblings you no longer talk to?

2. Who was your first love and what age did that happen?

3. What was the worst lie you ever told?

4. What is the hardest choice you have ever had to make and what was the outcome?

5. What do you feel is the most important ingredient to a friendship?

6. When was the most embarrassing moment of your life?

7. What is your best scar? Tell the story of how you got it.

8. Have you experienced a rift within your family caused by an inheritance?

9. Name three relatives you would not want to be stranded with on an island?

CHAPTER SIX – ENTERTAINMENT QUESTIONS

If there is ever a chapter people like to respond to and not get deeply personal, ENTERTAINMENT questions tend to bring out the opinions. Want to get a group talking quickly? Start here. Even if you grew up in an Amish community with no electricity, there is a universal ability for everyone to respond to questions about your favorite celebrities, TV shows, and movies (and for the record, if someone says they didn't have electricity growing up, then you can just start a string of questions about how they survived without Mork and Mindy).

What you will also see from these questions are strong, polar opposite responses from a medium to smaller group. Have a fan of the band RUSH? I'm sure you have an equally opposite feeling from that person's spouse. These questions can ignite a group in debate, so be prepared!

White Glue Questions (Entertainment)

1. If you could have had the starring role in one film already made, which movie would you pick?

2. If you were to perform in the circus, what would you do?

3. Name your favorite song.

4. Can you play any musical instrument right now and if not, what would you pick?

5. What was your favorite TV show when you were growing up?

6. What was your favorite TV show when you got home from school?

7. What is your favorite commercial?

8. What commercial annoys you the most?

9. If you had to be on a reality TV show, which one would you choose and why?

10. What kind of music do you like?

11. What was the first live concert you ever attended?

12. What is a song for which you thought you knew the words and later found out that you had them all wrong?

13. What's your favorite line from any movie?

14. What movie or TV show do you take guilty pleasure in watching?

15. If you had a band what would you name it?

16. What's your favorite karaoke song?

17. What is your favorite video game?

18. If you could listen to only one CD/Album/Record for the rest of your life, what would it be?

19. Who is your favorite actor/actress, and why?

20. What was the first record or CD that you bought?

21. What is your all-time favorite movie and why?

22. What type of music relaxes you the most?

23. If you auditioned for the reality show that involved singing, what song would you pick for your first song?

24. What is your favorite Disney song?

25. If you had to be a part of a reality show where you had to survive in the wilderness, whom from our group/team/office would you want to eliminate/remove first?

26. If you had to participate in a reality show as a business apprentice with all of your group/team participating, what two people from our group would end up in the finals?

27. What is your new favorite TV show in the past year?

28. What is recently discovered musical artist that you really enjoy listening to?

29. If you moved to Sesame Street, whom would you want as your neighbor?

30. Who is your favorite Muppet?

31. Of all of the Gilligan's Island characters, which are you most like and why?

32. If you could have any kind of a job in the entertainment industry, what do you think you would do best?

33. If you had your own talk show, who would your first three guests be?

34. Would you ever be on a reality TV show?

35. What is your favorite table or board game?

36. Have you ever been a participant in a parade and if so, what did you do?

37. What was your favorite 70s movie?

38. What was your favorite 80s movie?

39. What was your favorite 90s movie?

40. If you could live in any sitcom, what would it be?

41. What is your favorite cartoon movie?

42. If you could be a contestant on any game show, which one would you choose?

43. What is your favorite act at the circus?

44. What new movie are you most anxious to see released this year?

45. If you could attend any awards show, which would you choose?

46. What recent movie was so good that you want to buy it when it hits the stores?

47. Which video game console is your all-time favorite?

48. What three television channels would you and your significant other/roommate agree on as a favorite channel?

49. What is your favorite movie line?

50. What is the funniest movie you have ever seen?

51. What is the worst movie you have ever seen?

52. Who is your favorite comedian?

53. Have you ever called into a Talk Radio program?

54. How many hours a week do you watch TV?

55. How many times do you go to the movie theater each month?

56. What movie did you watch recently that you could consider being one of the greatest movies of all time?

57. Have you ever turned down tickets to a concert or sporting event and really regret not going?

58. When was the last time you went to a drive-in movie (if ever)?

59. What's the closest you've come to becoming a pop star/winning an Oscar?

60. If you were handed free opera tickets, would you go or sell them?

61. What is your favorite museum?

62. What artist in the last 100 years do you most admire?

63. Who is your favorite musical artist and have they ever won a Grammy?

64. What is the last concert you went to with your spouse/significant or kids?

65. What TV show would you want to come back "on air" since it ended?

66. What was the best "remake" movie where the remake was just as good or better than the original?

67. What was the best 'book to movie' you have ever seen?

Yellow Glue Questions (Entertainment)

1. If you were home on a rainy Sunday afternoon, what movie would you want to see on television?

2. I wish this year in entertainment were similar to the year _ _ _ _?

3. Name three celebrities you would want to be stranded with on an island?

4. Name three celebrities you would not want to be stranded with on an island?

5. What is the greatest movie you have NEVER seen?

6. What actor/actress would you like to play your life story in a movie?

7. What one television show are you embarrassingly addicted to?

8. What three television channels do you view most frequently?

9. Name one celebrity that has no right being a celebrity?

10. What is the saddest movie you have ever seen?

11. What is the scariest movie you've ever seen?

12. If you had to be a part of the reality TV show that called on you to travel the world with another person as your race partner, whom from our group/team/office would you pick as your partner?

13. If you could have a celebrity entourage with three celebrities, who would they be?

14. Describe the worst concert you ever attended (who, when, where).

15. What was the best concert you ever attended and where was it located?

16. What CD/tape/record do you wish was not in your collection?

17. Name the most famous person you've had a face-to-face encounter with.

Transparent Glue Questions (Entertainment)

1. What song reminds you most of a past or present relationship?

2. What famous person do you have feelings of hatred or disgust?

3. What celebrities' behavior most resembles your own?

4. What movie do you wish you never had seen because the content is now offensive?

5. What famous person do you know so well that you could call them right now?

6. What song most describes your life right now?

7. What movie makes you cry every time you see it?

CHAPTER SEVEN – GETTING PERSONAL QUESTIONS

Do you want to get to know how someone ticks? Start here.

This is the largest chapter of the book for a reason—because

everyone has a deep down desire to learn about others. This is

true in the business world as you try to sell them a new widget,

it's true on a team as you learn about the person sitting next to

you, and it's true on the car rental bus as you are being shuttled

from the airport to your waiting car. People are generally

curious and in a group setting they are even more curious about

you. Don't believe me? Think about this—if you are walking

down the street and you see someone approaching you wearing

his or her clothes backward, what is your first thought? Most

likely it's something like, "Why are they doing that?!?" If that

person happened to stop right next to you, do you think you

would ask why? Even an introvert like myself may courage up the strength to ask that one question. We are curious about others. Go get personal with these questions.

White Glue Questions (Getting Personal)

1. What do you own that sits in a display case?

2. Describe an interesting experience you had the last time your power went out.

3. What is set as the background on your phone (or computer)?

4. What do others say is your best personal characteristic?

5. If you had to enter a competition for the "Most Uselessly Unique Talent," what would your talent be?

6. What's your middle name and does it have a story behind it?

7. If you could only wear one color for the rest of your life, what would it be and why?

8. If you could have one super human power, what would it be?

9. Who have you been mistaken for and did you play along?

10. What do others say is your most attractive physical feature?

11. What traditional stereotype would you classify yourself as?

12. What kind of deodorant do you use?

13. If you have a birthmark, what does it look like and where is it located?

14. What is the best reward anyone can give you?

15. What can someone do to encourage you?

16. What is your favorite color and why?

17. If you had to lose one of your five senses (hearing, seeing, feeling, touch, taste), which one of them would you prefer to lose and why?

18. What was the worst smell you have ever smelled?

19. If you were on the cover of a magazine, which one would it be and why?

20. If you could be laid to rest anywhere, where would it be?

21. Name one thing that you couldn't live without.

22. What is your favorite guilty pleasure?

23. What's your favorite way to celebrate an accomplishment?

24. What kind of toothpaste do you use?

25. What do you keep in your wallet aside from money, cards and pictures?

26. How many places have you lived? (Share the number of physical residences and/or the number of cities)

27. How many pairs of shoes do you buy in a year?

28. What are two future hobbies you would like to start or learn about?

29. When do you feel old?

30. When do you feel like a younger version of your current age?

31. Which animal represents you the best and why?

32. What is your favorite way to express yourself and why?

33. Are there any interesting things your name spells with the letters rearranged?

34. Describe your worst day.

35. What are your three favorite smells?

What was the best smell you have ever smelled?

"THE SMELL OF A NEWBORN BABY, ESPECIALLY MY SON AFTER HE WAS BORN" – SUSAN D.

36. What do you have in your bag/wallet that best describes your personality?

37. Describe a word beginning with the first letter of your name that sums you up?

38. What is your biggest fear or phobia?

39. What is something you can do better than anyone else you know?

40. When are you at your silliest?

41. What childish things do you still do as an adult?

42. What is one major problem you had to solve this year?

43. If you can give advice on how to live life in one sentence, what would it be?

44. How do you express your anger to your enemy versus your best friends?

45. What is one particular day/night that you wanted to last forever?

46. What fantasy would you like to live out and why?

47. What was your scariest nightmare and when did you have it?

48. Tell us about the last time you had to ask for help.

49. What is your favorite thing to do in the summer?

50. What is your favorite thing to do in the winter?

51. What is your favorite thing to do in the fall?

52. What is your favorite thing to do in the spring?

53. You have to wear a T-shirt with one word on it for the rest of your life, which word do you choose?

54. Do you enjoy going shopping for clothes?

55. What do you enjoy shopping for?

56. What was the most mischievous April Fool's prank you've done?

57. If you had one free day to do anything you want, what would you do?

58. What can you always be found with?

59. When did you last write a handwritten letter?

60. On a scale from one to ten (ten the highest), how funny are you?

61. What celebrity do you most resemble?

62. What is the longest you have ever gone without taking a shower?

63. What is the most valuable item that has been stolen from you?

64. What website do you frequently visit for enjoyment?

65. Name your greatest phobia and when it started.

66. What is the most common compliment people have given you?

67. Where do you not mind waiting?

68. What issues are you sick of hearing about?

69. What is the best purchase you have ever made?

70. What is your favorite thing about being sick?

71. What luxury would you like to enjoy just once?

72. If the average person falls asleep in seven minutes...are you average, below, or above?

73. How good is your long-term memory, on a scale from one to ten (ten is the best)?

74. What is your favorite era in American History?

75. What irritates you the most in a social situation?

76. Do you have a place where you like to go and think?

77. Fill in the blank—I've never been able to _____.

78. How many minutes does it take for you to get ready in the morning?

79. On a scale of 1 to 10, how "hip" are you? (10 is most hip, 1 is least hip)

80. If you could attend any event, which one would it be?

81. If you could be a high-ranking officer in one of the armed forces, which one would you choose?

82. On a scale from one to ten, how proficient are you in typing?

83. If time was not a concern and you had lots of money, how would you decorate the outside of your home?

84. What one object in your home are you most embarrassed about owning?

85. What is the worst thing you have ever witnessed?

86. If I really wanted to annoy somebody, I would continually do what?

87. What was/is your best chance of becoming famous?

88. What color doesn't look good on you?

89. Name three things that you consider are "old-fashioned."

90. What is your most prized "autographed" item?

91. What was the last helpful thing you did?

92. Do you wash your hands every time you use a restroom?

93. What is your most favorite pair of shoes ever?

94. What is the most danger you've ever been in, and were you aware of it at the time?

95. If you got a tattoo what would you get and where would you put it?

96. What's the hardest thing you've ever done?

97. What do you keep in the trunk of your car?

98. How many rings before you answer the phone?

99. If you had to, what part of your body would you get pierced?

100.   Have you ever had a reoccurring dream?

101.   When did you last climb a tree?

102.   Do you tend to be a planner or a procrastinator?

103.   What is one store you will NEVER go to again?

104. What would you want your license plate to say on your current car?

105. If you got a tattoo on the back of your neck and it only contained words, what would it say?

106. What is your favorite quote?

107. Name a pet you have owned and how you came to name him/her.

108. What is your favorite animal?

109. What is your favorite time of day?

110. What is your favorite number?

111. I wish everyone would_____.

112. What past time period would you have liked to live?

113.   What do you love most about living in your country?

114.   If you could have a view of anything from your

bedroom, what would you chose?

115.   How many pillows do you like to sleep with at night?

116.   How much taller would you like to increase your height?

117.   What was the worst advice you ever gave?

118.   What worries you the most about your parents?

119.   If you need to drop some weight, what do you do?

120.   If you could be anything in the world, what would you

be and why?

121.   What is the scariest thing you have ever done for fun?

122.   How many bones have you broken in your life?

123.   If you could eliminate one thing you do each day in the bathroom so that you never had to do it again, what would it be?

124.   If you didn't have to get out of bed at a specific time in the morning, what time would you get up?

125.   Tell us about your most unusual hobby?

126.   When do you need or desire silence/no noise?

127.   What is the first thing you do when you wake up on a Saturday morning (or any other day off)?

128.   For what and how long did you stand in line the longest?

Yellow Glue Questions (Getting Personal)

1. Where was your favorite vacation as a child?

2. What do you hoard?

3. What doctor do you dread visiting the most?

4. If you were given 24 hours to live, what would you do?

5. What has been passed down to you from a previous generation?

6. What is something that nobody in the group knows about you?

7. What happened during your "15 minutes of fame?"

8. Who inspires you and how are you a little bit like them?

9. Based on something you've already done, how might you make it into the Guinness Book of World Records?

10. When was the last time you did something for the first time and what was it?

11. If you knew you could not fail, what would you do?

12. My biggest pet peeve is...

13. What is your worst personality characteristic?

14. What is one thing that you constantly think about?

15. What do you think is the best feeling in the world?

16. What is something you have that is of sentimental value?

17. Can you comfortably eat in a restaurant by yourself?

18. Can you go to a movie by yourself?

19. If you could snap your fingers and appear somewhere else, where would you be?

20. What specific thing have you done that impressed yourself?

21. Where would you like to retire and why?

22. What is the craziest (or stupidest) thing you have ever done?

23. Who has been the biggest inspiration in your life and why?

24. Tell two truths and one lie about yourself to the others in your group.

25. If I wasn't afraid I would _____ .

26. If given a chance to get back at something/someone during the past, what will be that time and why?

27. What is something you have lost that you have never found, or were tremendously relieved when you did find it?

28. If you had the opportunity to live one year of your life over again, which year would you choose?

29. Describe in details at least two of your personalities or how others would describe them.

30. If you were blind for the rest of your life, what would you miss seeing the most?

31. What is your most disappointing moment in life?

32. When have you laughed the hardest?

33. When have you cried the hardest?

34. What is one thing people would be surprised to learn about you?

35. If you could only have one thing on a deserted island what would it be?

36. Is there a story behind your name?

37. What takes you out of your comfort zone?

38. Sitting alone in a big field, looking at stars, what do you think/feel?

39. Which one physical feature would you change if you could?

40. What scares you the most?

41. What are you thankful for?

42. What was the best year of your life and why?

43. Using only one word, name something significant about your life today.

44. If your house were on fire, what one thing would you take (assuming your family and pets were already safe)?

45. If you could spend your last hours of life with anyone, doing anything, whom would you choose and what would you do?

46. Have you ever had the police called on you?

47. If you could take back something hurtful you've once said to someone, what would it be?

48. What is the best gift anyone's ever given you?

49. Tell us one of the worst fights you ever got into?

50. What questions would you NOT like others to ask you?

51. Give us a situation where you felt life had been unfair to you?

52. What are your goals for living?

53. When people look at me, they would never guess that I

_____.

54. What was your last thought before going to sleep?

55. What is your first thought in the morning?

56. When was the last time you had a dream and what was it about?

57. If you were to die tomorrow, what would your tombstone say?

58. If you could erase one day in history which one would it be and why?

59. What is something unexpected that has changed about you in the last few years?

60. Have you ever gotten a black eye and how did it happen?

61. Have you ever given someone a black eye and how did it happen?

62. What's the coldest you have ever been in your life?

63. How often do you journal your thoughts or ideas and what topic is a frequent entry?

64. What is your best chance of becoming famous?

65. What two words describe your lifestyle?

66. Fill in the blank—I would like to be known as the world's greatest _____.

67. If you knew a nuclear war would begin in two hours, what would you do?

68. What do you consider your most prized object (family excluded)?

69. Do you talk more than you listen?

70. What do you consider the worst household chore?

71. What are you thankful you're not doing right now?

72. What do you hate sharing with people?

73. Would you let anyone in this group eat off your plate?

74. Name 10 things you do every day.

75. If you could change one event in the course of world history, what would it be?

76. On a scale from 1 to 10 (10 high), how much do you trust people?

77. What is the most memorable "thank you" you ever received?

78. What are you most proud of (outside of family/kids)?

79. On a scale from 1 to 10 (10 highest), how often do you stereotype people?

80. Have you been handling things proactively or reactively lately?

81. What do you dislike about failure and what can you learn from it?

82. Share an experience where you felt out of place.

83. What's changed in your life since we last saw (or spoke) to each other?

84. What was your biggest accomplishment last month?

85. If you have children, what is the meaning of their middle name?

86. Explain how the people around you are better at their job than you?

87. Name three presidents you would want to be stranded with on an island?

88. What life lesson can you never forget because it is associated with a great story?

89. I've done _____ in a movie theater?

90. How do you respond in a crisis situation?

91. What is the one memorable item that got thrown away?

Transparent Glue Questions (Getting Personal)

1. What do you think the most ultimate gift to the world?

2. Name a turning point in your life that makes you smile/cry.

3. How would you like to be remembered?

4. Where do you see yourself in ten years?

5. What's your passion?

6. What is one secret that you haven't told anyone?

7. What is the best thing you have done in your life?

8. When was the last time you cried and why?

9. Name a major life experience that made you who you are today?

10. What could you do to improve your life?

11. What's the most important thing to you in life?

12. What's it like to be on the other side of me? (Or what's it like to engage with me?)

13. If nobody were watching, what would you do?

14. What is your greatest addiction?

15. What life-altering change have you been meaning to do?

16. Do you have any implants or unnatural attachments to your body?

17. What are you wrestling with in your thought life?

18. In what area of your life do you need a new "starting point?"

19. What or who do you miss the most?

20. What are your top priorities?

21. Do you seek out accountability or do you tend to avoid it?

22. What attitude adjustments would help the way you view suffering?

23. What have your learned from your most recent personal failure?

24. How well do you receive and accept instruction?

25. What do you consume?

26. Who do you spend time with?

27. Who do you spend time with outside of your profession?

28. Describe your current season of life.

29. How depleted are you right now?

30. How long has it been since you have felt fully replenished?

31. What does life feel like when your energy bucket is filled all the way to the top?

32. What does life feel like when your energy bucket is completely empty?

33. What fills your energy bucket?

34. What in your life right now is giving you energy and passion?

35. Who in your life has the permission to say the hard things to you that you need to hear?

36. Who is currently your mentor or coach and what are you discovering about yourself?

37. Who are you currently mentoring or coaching and if no one, why not?

38. What are your limitations and potentials?

CHAPTER EIGHT – FOOD QUESTIONS

Where do most group conversations begin? If you grew up in a big family, the dinner table was THE place for loud discussions, questions, and the central hub to the entire house. Because food is typically served at the table, these questions are a great starting point for breaking the uncomfortable tension when everyone sits down. Who doesn't have a favorite food, worst restaurant, or a favorite dessert? If you are having a dinner party, these questions are a great appetizer!

White Glue Questions (Food)

1. What was the weirdest food you have ever eaten?

2. What is your favorite weird food combination?

3. What's the best dinner you have ever eaten?

4. If you were on death row, what would you request as your last meal?

5. If you could only go to one restaurant for the next five years, which would you choose?

6. What is the best dessert you have ever eaten?

7. What is your favorite breakfast?

8. What is your favorite candy as an adult?

9. What is your favorite candy as a child?

10. What are your favorite pizza toppings?

11. Name your top three favorite pop/sodas.

12. If you had to give up one food forever, what would it be?

13. What is your favorite ice cream flavor?

14. What is your favorite restaurant and why?

15. If you could have one thing to drink before you died what would it be and why?

16. What is your favorite cheese?

17. What is your idea of a great dessert?

18. What is your favorite dish at an Italian restaurant?

19. What are your three favorite spices?

20. List the food items you take at a salad bar.

21. What item do you always skip at a salad bar?

22. What is your favorite soup?

23. What is your favorite homemade Italian dish?

24. What is your favorite kind of pie?

25. Do you prefer eating the frosting of the cupcake or the cupcake first?

26. Explain in details how you eat corn on the cob.

27. What is the best or most interesting food buffet you have ever seen?

28. What is your favorite fruit?

29. What is your favorite form of potato?

30. What is the most expensive restaurant you've ever been to?

31. What's your favorite type of cookie?

32. How many slices of pizza could you consume if you pushed your limits?

33. Aside from lettuce, what are your two favorite salad

    ingredients?

34. What is your favorite kind of cereal?

35. If you owned a restaurant, what type of food would you

    serve?

36. What is the most exotic food you have ever eaten?

37. If fat calories, cholesterol, etc. weren't an issue, what three

    name-brand foods would you feast on?

38. Who in our group/team/office would most likely win a

    hotdog-eating contest?

39. What is your favorite kind of donut or pastry?

40. What is your favorite flavor of jellybeans?

41. What is your favorite greasy appetizer and from what restaurant?

42. What would you generally order at the food counter in a movie theater?

43. When you are eating bad and enjoying every minute of it, what are you usually eating?

44. What is the most memorable "non-candy" treat you got as a child and when have you last had it as an adult?

45. What would be a perfect topping(s) for a hamburger?

46. What is your favorite kind of sandwich?

47. Where would be the perfect lunch spot to eat if you wanted to get away from people?

48. Where would be the perfect lunch spot to catch up with a friend?

49. Recommend a restaurant that has been recommended to you, but you have never tried.

50. How many chicken wings can you eat in one sitting?

51. What is your favorite restaurant in your "hometown?"

52. What veggie can you eat now, but could never as a kid?

Yellow Glue Questions (Food)

1. Which recommended restaurant was the biggest letdown?

2. Can you go a year without eating any meat?

3. Can you go a year without eating any chocolate?

4. Where do you feel is the best sandwich in town?

5. Where do you feel is the best pizza in town?

6. If you were to choose to make dinner for a very special guest, what would you cook?

7. Name one common food item that you refuse to eat.

8. What is the first word that comes to your mind when you think of a coffee shop?

9. If you could bathe in a vat of any drink or food item, what would you choose?

10. If you could own any restaurant, but know that you could never eat there again, what would you choose?

11. If you had to eat in a restaurant by yourself, what would you do to pass the time between ordering the food and eating it?

12. What is one restaurant you will NEVER go to again?

Transparent Glue Questions (Food)

1. Do you struggle with eating too much?

2. What food or drink will cause you to fall off of your diet?

3. Do you stereotype people who eat too much?

4. Do you stereotype people who drink too much?

5. Who in your family eats or drinks too much and needs to seek outside help?

6. Describe a time where you confronted someone who was drinking too much.

7. Tell us about the first time you had too many "adult beverages."

8. What food have you banned from your diet?

CHAPTER NINE – TRAVEL QUESTIONS

This topic called "travel" normally generates two unique

responses when asked in a group setting. The first group is what

I called the "dreamers" where the conversation drifts off to an

unknown distant future. These long, deep thoughts about exotic

locations have been thought about in details. Dreams of

retirement and exploring the depths of the world evolve from

the simplest question.

The other group, called "team drudgery" have flown all around

the world, have one billion frequent flier miles stored up, are

members of every possible airline club, but find travel not a

pleasurable event. They would much rather spend time at home

or a quick drive to a beach instead of being locked into a flying

tube for 10 hours (not including the fun of security lines and flight delays!). In either case, these are great questions to ask to a group of business folks at your next conference.

White Glue Questions (Travel)

1. What mountain would you want to climb someday?

2. What do you keep in the trunk of your car when you travel?

3. If you could plan your ultimate vacation, where would you go?

4. If you could fly to a different time zone, which one would you fly to and why?

5. What is one of the strangest southern USA expressions you have heard?

6. Would you rather go the short way slow or take the long way fast if you got to your destination at the same amount of time?

7. Would you live in space if you could never come back to earth?

8. If you had to move out of this country, what country would you move to and why?

9. If you could travel anywhere in the world, where would you go?

10. If you could live anywhere for one year, all expenses paid, where would you live?

11. If you could drive, ride, or fly anything to get to your workplace, what would you choose?

12. If you could be anywhere, doing anything right now, where would you be and what would you be doing?

13. If you could time travel, where would you go, and what would you do?

14. If you could instantly become fluent in another language, what would that language be and why?

15. How many languages do you speak?

16. How many auto accidents have you been in?

17. What was the farthest you have ever traveled?

18. Where and how long was the farthest road trip you have ever taken?

19. If you could visit any place in the world for a month with only allowed a backpack for your personal belongings, where would it be and why?

20. What is the worst method of travel?

21. What is the best method of travel?

22. How many countries have you traveled to?

23. What is the longest period of time you have spent in car?

24. If you could have an all-expense-paid week vacation from work, where would you go?

25. What is the first thing that comes to your mind when you think of Australia?

26. What is your favorite thing about the beach?

27. Where and how long was the longest you have ever been delayed at an airport?

28. What national monument or park have you always wanted to visit?

29. If you could change one thing about airlines to make your flight more enjoyable, what would it be?

30. When you are a passenger in a car, what is the worst thing a driver can do?

31. What is your favorite city that you've traveled to?

32. Where is the most beautiful place you've ever been?

33. Where did your family go for vacations in the summer when you were young?

34. What is the biggest tourist attraction in the USA that you have not been to or seen?

35. What would you list as the two biggest tourist attractions in (enter your city)?

36. What do you feel should be the personal and public policy on seat reclining in airplanes?

37. When traveling by car, what is the worst stretch of road to be on a "road trip?"

38. When traveling by car, how do you pass the time if you are by yourself?

39. When traveling by car, how do you pass the time if you are with someone else?

40. What is the longest you have traveled with someone you did not know very well?

41. When traveling by car, what is the best stretch of road for a road trip?

42. What was the cheapest gas price you can remember for one gallon/liter?

43. If you could add one feature to your car, what would you choose?

44. If you could travel to anywhere in the US by yourself for a long weekend, where would you go and why?

45. Where is the best vacation spot for kids?

46. What would you say has been the best vacation of all times?

47. Outside of your own vacation experiences, describe the best vacation that someone you know experienced.

Yellow Glue Questions (Travel)

1. Where was your favorite vacation as a child?

2. Describe your worst experience as a passenger in an airplane.

3. Describe the most interesting person you have met while traveling on an airplane.

4. What is the longest flight you have been on?

5. If you were traveling around the world, what two people would you want as your companions?

6. When you were growing up, what is the worst thing that has happened during one of your vacations?

7. Could you ever live overseas for a year?

8. Could you ever live overseas for a decade?

9. Where is that dream vacation location in which you have never visited?

10. What do you typically do on a vacation?

11. What was your worst vacation experience?

12. Describe the last time you got into an auto accident and what was the outcome.

13. How many times have you gotten out of a speeding ticket?

14. How many times have you gotten a speeding ticket?

15. Have you ever traveled somewhere and said, "I could not live here?"

16. What is the most interesting incident you've had at airport security since 9/11/2001?

17. When was your worst or dramatic car trouble story?

18. Name three things that make you quietly laugh when you hear someone is moving to (insert city or state here)?

Transparent Glue Questions (Travel)

1. Describe the best vacation your parents had no idea that you took?

2. What is the most memorable vacation you had as a child?

3. Have you ever dated someone after meeting him or her while vacationing?

4. Have you ever been arrested or incarcerated while traveling?

5. If you could snap your fingers and be anywhere in the world for five seconds then immediately return, where would you go? (Would your answer change if you were there for one minute, one hour, or one day?)

CHAPTER TEN – SPORTS QUESTIONS

This topic does not go deep. It's also suited perfect for the guys.

Gals—if you start answering or even start asking these

questions, you will become very popular with the opposite sex.

White Glue Questions (Sports)

1. What's your favorite sport to play?

2. What is your favorite sport to watch and which team of that

   sport do you cheer for?

3. If you could be a professional at any sport, what would it

   be?

4. If you could go bowling with any three people—dead or alive—who would you choose and why?

5. If you were a pro wrestler, what would your name be?

6. When was the last time you went bowling?

7. If you could perform in the Olympics, what sport would you pick and why?

8. What is your favorite or most memorable NFL Super Bowl Commercial?

9. If you were on a professional sports team, what number would you wear on your uniform?

10. What is your favorite event in the Summer Olympics?

11. What is your favorite event in the Winter Olympics?

12. If you can be recognized as the greatest athlete in any sport, which sport would it be?

13. What sport have you watched that you have no idea what the rules are to play the game?

14. Who do you feel is the most admired athlete of all time?

15. Outside of your favorite team(s), what athlete do you secretly admire?

16. If you could coach any professional sports team, which one would it be?

17. Fill in the blank—I could probably bench press _____ pounds.

18. What is the most athletic activity you have ever participated in?

19. Who would be the ping-pong champion of your group/team/office?

20. What is your favorite professional sports stadium?

21. Do you do anything special for the NCAA basketball tournament held every March?

22. Which person on your team/group/office is the most distracted by the NCAA basketball tournament?

23. What are your two favorite sports teams?

24. What is your favorite athletic activity?

25. If you were given 100 chances to throw a dart at the bulls-eye, how many times would you hit it?

26. If you were a hunting fanatic, what animal would you hang from your wall as a trophy?

27. If you were given the opportunity for free skydiving lessons would you take them?

28. What would be your average score when you went bowling?

29. What do you enjoy more during the NFL SuperBowl: the game, the commercials, or the food?

30. How late would you stay up to watch your favorite sports team or player?

31. Have you ever jumped out of a plane?

32. If you had to go outside today and run, how far could you go?

33. Describe the best seats you have ever had during a sporting event.

34. What is the most you have ever paid to attend a sporting event?

35. Which team is your archrival?

36. Name your three favorite teams from any sport and how many winning championships they have had during your lifetime.

37. Could you run five miles today and how long would it take you?

38. If given the chance, what would you change with the game of baseball?

39. If given a chance, what would you change with the game of kickball?

40. How could you combine baseball and soccer into a new sport?

41. What two sports combined would make a great new sport?

Yellow Glue Questions (Sports)

1. What sports team did you root for as a child, but no longer have that alliance?

2. What was the most crushing defeat you have ever experienced in sports?

3. Who was the greatest cheater in sports?

4. In sports, what would be worthy of a lifetime ban?

5. If you could go back in time, what sport would you have tried while in high school?

6. Do you ever keep in touch with any of your former coaches?

7. If you could be the "General Manager" of your favorite professional sports team and have the power to reverse any trade that happened over the past 10 years, which trade would you reverse?

8. Which sport would you be most embarrassed to be known as the greatest?

9. Which athlete is your most respected?

10. If you could invest in any sport and/or team for only the next 10 years, which one would give the biggest return on your investment?

11. What is your personally greatest sporting achievement?

12. Which athlete is your most despised over all other athletes in that particular sport?

CHAPTER ELEVEN – HOLIDAY QUESTIONS

Happy Holidays? In some cases, not so much! I can't help but flash back to the classic Chevy Chase movie called "Christmas Vacation" and think about that crazy adventure of how their holiday celebration unfolded. We laugh about his follies with family, but for some people that movie is not too far from the truth. Holidays can bring out the best and worst of families, so these questions tend to bring out some great big stories of years past.

White Glue Questions (Holidays)

1.   When trick-or-treating as a kid, was there any kind of candy that you didn't like to get?

2. What is the weirdest gift you have ever received?

3. What is your favorite holiday season?

4. If you were attending a Halloween party, what would your costume be and why?

5. What single day is your favorite of any holiday?

6. Who in your group/team is most likely to go all out on a Halloween costume?

7. What is your favorite Christmas scent?

8. In your opinion, how many inches (if any) would be the ideal accumulation of snow for a white Christmas Day?

9. What is the longest period of time you've ever left your tree up after the Christmas holiday?

10. What is the longest period of time you've ever left your outdoor lights up after the Christmas holiday?

11. Have you ever given someone a fruitcake for Christmas?

12. What is one of your favorite Fourth of July memories?

13. When do you start listening to Christmas or Holiday music?

14. When do you typically put up the Christmas tree?

15. When do you typically start hanging Christmas lights outside?

16. When is the last day you can have your Christmas lights turned on outside?

17. When do you start shopping for Christmas?

18. When did you have the best New Year's Eve?

19. How far would your travel for a New Year's Eve party?

20. How was Christmas celebrated at your house when you were 10?

21. What was the best (or worst) "White Elephant" gift received or given?

22. What could you not eat at a Thanksgiving dinner?

23. Thinking back to your childhood, what is the one memory you have about Halloween?

24. Do you set yearly goals on or around the New Year?

25. What is the best costume you have ever worn for Halloween?

26. As a child, what could you guarantee was in your Easter basket (if you got one)?

27. What is the best fireworks display you have ever seen?

28. For those "Black Friday" shoppers, what was the best deal you ever got?

29. If you could have your way, what would be the official candy of Christmas?

30. On a scale of one to ten (with one being in perfect order and ten being an intertwined, out-of-control mess), how tangled are your Christmas lights when you first take them out each year?

31. What tends to be the last gift you purchase each year?

32. How many costumes do you own today that you could wear for Halloween?

33. Who is the hardest person to shop for on your Christmas list this year?

34. What present did you purchase for someone else, in which you are most excited to see them open it?

35. What is the best way to celebrate New Year's Eve?

36. Would you go to a "Haunted House" during the Halloween season?

Yellow Glue Questions (Holidays)

1. Think back over your lifetime, what was the best New Year's celebration you were a part of?

2. At Christmastime, which do you honestly enjoy more— giving or receiving?

3. Has your "best Christmas ever" been within the past five years, 6-10 years, 10-25 years, or 26-50 years?

4. Who is the one person you don't want to get stuck sitting next to at the family Christmas party?

5. What is your favorite memory of Christmas past?

6. What was the most unique gift you got (or gave) this holiday season?

7. How is Christmas typically celebrated at your house now?

8. What was your worst Christmas present ever?

9. What was your best Christmas present ever?

10. Is there a holiday tradition you want to start this year?

Transparent Glue Questions (Holidays)

1. What unhappy memory do you have of Christmas past?

2. Are you reminded of anyone when a certain holiday approaches?

3. What is the worst action you were a part of during a Halloween scare?

4. Are there certain holidays you avoid completely?

5. Has someone or something robbed you of experiencing the joy during a holiday season?

CHAPTER TWELVE – DATING, MARRIAGE, & RELATIONSHIP QUESTIONS

For some people, this is the first chapter they want to start with...especially in the early stages of a relationship. Though these questions are designed for a group setting, they can also be used to learn about a potential lifelong partner. Or better yet, could be crucial in figuring out who is that "special one" that mama would approve of.

Asking the questions and experiencing the answer can be a very intimate experience. If there was any time to pay full attention to the answer, (yes I am talking to those A.D.D. folks!), these questions would be the most important.

For a small portion of people, these questions can bring up a hurtful past. Tread carefully here, as some of these issues have not been stirred up for many years. Listen, listen, listen is the best advice for these questions.

White Glue Questions (Relationships)

1. What is the best or worst pick up line you have ever heard?

2. How many dates do you go on with someone before you introduce them to your parents?

3. Would you rather spend the rest of your life in love with a rich person or a poor person?

4. Describe your dream wedding where money is no option.

5. What is the first thing you notice about the opposite sex?

6. Describe your ideal romantic date.

7. Name one important characteristic you look for in someone you consider a friend.

8. If there was only one item left of your most favorite things to eat, would you let your significant other have it or would you eat it yourself?

9. Have you ever said something to your significant other that you regretted, but were glad to have gotten the topic of conversation started?

10. Would you ever use a dating service (match.com, e-harmony, etc.) to find someone?

11. What is the greatest conflict between men and women?

12. At what age did you have your first boyfriend/girlfriend?

13. Where is the most romantic place to meet your true love?

14. Who was your first big crush?

15. If you could date any celebrity, who would it be and why?

16. Recommend a date night that costs less than $10.

17. If you have kids, what do your kids do today that you would NEVER have done at their age?

18. What outside chore does your spouse hate the most?

19. Could you date (or marry) someone who is shorter than you?

20. Could you date (or marry) someone who is a foot taller than you?

21. Who was your best friend as a child and why?

22. Who was your best friend as a teenager and why?

23. Who is your best friend now and why?

24. Have you ever been married before?

Yellow Glue Questions (Relationships)

1. What was one of the worst ways you reacted to a declaration of love?

2. Have you ever lied about your age?

3. Have you ever lied about your weight?

4. What would you leave in your will for the person you care about the most?

5. Would you rather meet the love of your life, knowing he/she will die within a year, or go without meeting him/her?

6. Where did you meet your mate?

7. What was the most embarrassing thing you have done while on a date?

8. What do you look for in a friend?

9. What type of partner would you choose for yourself?

10. What obstacles do you find when trying to become a close friend to someone of the opposite sex?

11. Where were you when you had your first kiss?

12. What person have you always wondered whether or not they liked you?

13. If the plane you were flying in were about to crash, whom would you want sitting next to you?

14. What is the best way to lose a friend?

15. What outfit or piece of clothing do you like to see your spouse/partner wear?

16. When was the last time you went on a date with your spouse (just the two of you)?

17. Answer for your spouse –what would be the best date night experience?

18. What store would you buy a gift certificate for your spouse?

19. Who is the person you get along with the best from your spouse's side of the family?

20. What child in your neighborhood do you feel is not being raised properly?

21. What happened this summer that will become a long lasting memory for your kids (good or bad)?

22. Describe the one chore in the house that your spouse does NOT like to do.

23. Describe the perfect vacation...from your spouse's point of view.

Transparent Glue Questions (Relationships)

1. What was your longest relationship and why did it end?

2. Have you ever been in love?

3. How many people have you been in love with over your lifetime?

4. Have you ever sent a picture of yourself to someone, which did not represent the current truth about who you are?

5. Could you take a vow of celibacy for a year?

6. Could you date someone 20 years younger than yourself?

CHAPTER THIRTEEN – BUSINESS, CAREER, EDUCATION QUESTIONS

If you are sitting in your office contemplating if this "Group Glue" will work for your team, then start here. These questions are a perfect starter for the business setting or outing while keeping it "safe" for those not wanting to go too personal. Be warned, that once you start asking these questions, your team may start to enjoy getting to know each other better and you will forced to dive into questions from one of the other chapters.

White Glue Questions (Career)

1.   What was your hourly rate for your first job?

2. What companies tend to always grab your attention?

3. Which brands inspire you?

4. What is the worst volunteer (unpaid) job you ever had?

5. What was in your high school locker?

6. Who do you know personally that has the coolest job/career?

7. Who has a job that you still do not know what they do even after they have explained it in detail?

8. If you could have any job in the world, which one would you want?

9. If you were tasked to put something in a cereal box as a promotion, and your job depended on its success, what would you pick?

10. What was your first job where someone paid you other than your parents?

11. If you could attend any college, free of charge, what college would that be and what major would you pursue?

12. Name two words you always seem to spell incorrectly.

13. What is the worst job/occupation in the world?

14. If you could own one type of retail store, what would it be?

15. On a scale from 1 to 10 (10 highest), how hard of a worker are you?

16. Who in our group/team/office would be the best at handling the heat of a press conference?

17. Who in our group/team/office would you choose to negotiate a raise for you?

18. On a scale from 1 to 10 (10 highest), how proficient are you in car repair?

19. If you were a teacher, what subject would you teach?

20. What is college really good for?

21. How many work-related parties or events do you attend every year that are not located in your office building?

22. Do customer comments, including criticism, lead to real changes in your policies and procedures at work?

23. What specific customer in your line of work do you "vent" about the most?

24. Have you ever gone to a job interview where you felt underdressed?

25. Does a college degree make a difference in the work place?

26. Do you agree with the statement that the longer you stay put at a job that doesn't satisfy, the less likely it is to evolve into something satisfying?

27. What makes a job satisfying?

28. Do people treat different kinds of customers differently at your workplace?

29. What do you like least when the boss is away from the office?

30. What do you like most when the boss is away from the office?

31. What kind of business would you love to start?

32. What were your best/worst subjects in school and what subjects would you want to learn now?

33. Who was your favorite teacher and why?

34. What is the best or most interesting class you have ever

    taken in high school, college or graduate school?

35. When you were in elementary school, what was your

    favorite activity at recess?

36. What clubs where you involved in during high school and

    college?

37. Did you ever consider becoming a teacher and why?

38. Do you remember your ACT or SAT scores and how many

    times did it take you to get your best score?

39. How often do you do work on Saturday for your current

    employer?

40. How often do you do work on Sunday for your current employer?

41. What is your absolute favorite part of your work day?

42. What is one of your favorite things to do on Friday afternoon at work?

43. What do you waste your time doing?

44. What is your favorite way to waste time at work without getting caught?

45. What is your concept of a fruitful day?

46. What was the best conference or convention you attended that was paid for by your employer?

Yellow Glue Questions (Career)

1. What is the worst job/occupation at your current place of employment?

2. If you could go back and change your career path what would you be doing now?

3. What is your dream job?

4. If you could be the president of any corporation, which would you choose?

5. What is your most distinct memory of your first week at your current job?

6. If you were to rank all of the people in your high school graduating class based on how successful they are, or are going to be, where would you fall?

7. Name one thing you learned over the past year that amazes you that you never knew before?

8. If you could restart your career right now, in your current line of work, what would you do different?

9. What career did your parents want you to get into?

10. If your company said they would write you a check to quit your job, what is the lowest amount you would accept to never work there again?

11. If someone were going to come along and put your current employer (or your current business) out of business, what would they do to achieve this?

12. What is the worst grade you ever received?

13. If you had one extra hour of free time a day, how would you use it?

14. Have you ever felt that someone else has taken credit for your work?

15. Have you ever had a "Rudy moment" where you worked hard for weeks/months/years for a small victory and was it worth it?

16. What is one thing you've learned about your job in the last year?

17. If your boss told you to take the day off today, what specifically would you go do?

18. When was the last time you had to speak in front of 100 or more people?

19. What was the largest group you have ever had the chance to speak in front of?

Transparent Glue Questions (Career)

1. Have you ever cheated on a test in school?

2. What would you say to a peer/friend who was just going through the motions of the job and it was impacting your workload?

3. What can you do different with five percent of your waking time each day (~48 minutes) that would make a lifetime impact?

4. Could you turn your hobby into a career and, if so, then what would need to happen?

5. What would make you change careers?

6. What will you be doing "careerwise" when you are 70?

7. Have you ever stolen anything from an employer?

8. Tell us about a time when you had to resign from a job.

CHAPTER FOURTEEN – GOD, FAITH, & SPIRITUALITY QUESTIONS

If you are looking for the deepest questions, start here. Religion is a deeply personal topic that is rarely brought up in casual setting or around a business luncheon. Questions about God and Faith have divided countries, started wars, and in some households are taboo to even discuss. You will not find many "White Glue" questions in this chapter, but you will have plenty of deep questions to understand where a person stands on their Faith. Careful consideration should be given to these questions, as they tend to have some very sharp opinions.

White Glue Questions (Faith)

1. Do you believe in ghosts or evil spirits?

2. If you could ask Noah (From the Biblical story of Noah's Ark) one question, what would it be?

3. Do you believe in angels?

4. What faith or religion did you parents pass on to you?

5. What types of churches or places of worship have you visited?

6. How many spiritual books do you own?

7. Who is the most spiritual person you would consider a friend?

8. Who in your family is the most religious?

9. What is your earliest childhood memory of church?

10. How often do you pray?

11. Do you believe in luck or karma?

12. If you were looking for peace, where would you go?

Yellow Glue Questions (Faith)

1. When was the last time you prayed and what did you pray about?

2. What person in the Bible do you most closely identify with?

3. If you could meet anyone from the Bible (besides Jesus Christ) who would it be and what would you ask them?

4. Where would you be willing to serve as a missionary?

5. If you could bring one person back from the dead who would it be and why?

6. What would you do if you really liked someone and after a while of hanging out you discovered that they did not believe in God?

7. If today were the day you see your "Maker," what would you want them to say as a welcome?

8. If there is a hell, where is it?

9. How is it between God and you right now?

10. Which song brings you the most internal peace?

11. Do you believe in reincarnation?

12. When do you feel aware of God's presence (if ever)?

13. If your entrance into a peaceful eternity were based on your actions of goodness, would you be let in?

14. If you die in your sleep, what happens next?

15. If in this world there is a battle of good versus evil, which is winning?

16. Have you ever been afraid of a spiritual being?

Transparent Glue Questions (Faith)

1. Have you ever been mad at God?

2. What is the most outrageous thing you've done in the name of religion?

3. If you were God, the first thing you would do is

   _____.

4. If you could ask God one question, what would it be?

5. How does God feel about you?

6. If you can thank God for one thing in your life, what would it be?

7. What is the #1 prayer need for you this week?

8. How has your relationship with God been changing?

9. What is the one thing you really need to hear from God right now?

10. If you could ask God one question about the Bible, what would it be?

11. What do you think matters most to God?

12. Is there anything you have done that would be considered unforgiveable?

13. Has anything happened to you that you would consider is unforgiveable?

14. When you head hits the pillow at night, are you at peace?

15. What is the purpose of life?

CHAPTER FIFTEEN – PEOPLE QUESTIONS

This is a fun chapter to learn about connections. Real

connections to people you may know or desired connections to

those from the past, current, or future. You can learn a lot

about someone based on the people they know, people they

consider friends, and those people they want to meet.

White Glue Questions (People)

1. If you could spend 15 minutes with any living person, who

    would it be and why?

2. If you could meet anyone from history, who would you

    meet and why?

3. If you could switch bodies with a certain celebrity, who would it be and why?

4. What famous person do you know or have met personally?

5. If you had to be handcuffed to one person for an entire month, who would it be?

6. Is there one historical figure you would like to have a discussion with and what would you talk about?

7. Name two people you would most like to stand next to in a photograph?

8. What is the first thing you notice when you meet someone?

9. Who in your team/group/office is the least likely to have had a prison record?

10. Who in your team/group/office is the most afraid of public

 speaking?

11. Who in your team/group/office should be in charge of

 organizing a party?

12. Who in your team/group/office would be the best

 performer at karaoke night?

13. Who in your team/group/office are you most like?

14. If you had to cover your bedroom with wallpaper displaying

 someone's face, which face would you choose?

15. Among the people in your group/team/office, whom would

 you trust most to hold a spare key to your house?

16. If someone at a gas station walked up and asked you for one dollar to get home because he forgot his wallet, would you be willing to give him the money?

17. If someone at a gas station walked up and asked you for $10 to get home because he forgot his wallet, would you be willing to give him the money?

18. What things can you say to make people feel better when there is a problem?

19. Have you ever put together a big surprise for someone else?

20. If your spouse forced you to buy a present for your mother-in-law, what would you buy her?

21. Who was the most famous person from your hometown?

22. What country seems to have the happiest people?

Yellow Glue Questions (People)

1. Who do you admire the most?

2. What historical figure do you most admire?

3. Have you run into situation where someone was not
    "playing by the rules" and had a short return/gain, but in
    the long run it hurt them in some way?

4. Who do you think killed John F. Kennedy?

5. Who is your hero?

6. Do you have a set of standard opening questions when you
    meet someone new?

7. Has anyone asked you something unique when you first met him or her that caught you off-guard?

8. When have you been surprised by something said in the last two weeks?

9. Name the first person that comes to your mind whom you feel is lying (anyone in the world).

Transparent Glue Questions (People)

1. What is something remarkable that you have witnessed a friend do?

2. What is something remarkable that you have witnessed a stranger do?

3. Explain why some people don't get along with you.

4. What group of people do you have a hard time relating to?

CHAPTER SIXTEEN – TECHNOLOGY QUESTIONS

Are you a gadget geek? There seems to be two camps in regards to technology—those who embrace it (and quickly) and those who resist it. Many battles have been raised in break rooms across the world with loud, passionate discussions on the following:

Microsoft vs. Apple

iPhone vs. Android

Canon vs. Nikon

Dell vs. Toshiba

The battle goes on and on. If you are in a room with technology folks, this is a great chapter to get the group to bind or battle each other.

White Glue Questions (Technology)

1. Name three things you think will become obsolete in ten years.

2. What one thing (Modern convenience) you could not live without that was created or developed in the last 20 years?

3. What one thing (Modern convenience) you could not live without that was created or developed in the last 10 years?

4. What one thing (Modern convenience) you could not live without that was created or developed in the last five years?

5. Has modern technology enhanced or complicated your life?

6. How often do you bid on eBay (or some other bidding website) and if so, what was the last item you won?

7. If you could invent a gadget what would it be and why?

8. How many times per day do you check to see if you have voicemail at home or work?

9. How many times per day do you check your cell phone for any sort of messages?

10. Should cell phone usage be allowed during commercial airline travel and why?

11. What is the most aggravating automated phone system you have had to endure?

12. When a new product comes on the market are you one of the first to buy it or do you wait to see how others receive it before buying?

13. How many personal phone calls do you make each day?

14. If you could add one feature to your mobile phone, what would it be?

15. Which gadget has changed your life?

16. Which gadget have you never fully learned how to use?

17. Have you ever posted a video online to YouTube.com or some other online site?

Yellow Glue Questions (People)

1. What one thing (modern convenience) could you not live without?

2. What is the next big thing in technology?

3. Have you ever invested in technology and lost?

4. If we searched the Internet for your name what would we find?

5. Have you ever posted a comment/question into an online forum?

6. What have you contributed to the Internet that has garnered the most attention from others?

7. Who have you "unfriended" or dropped as a "connection" from any social media website?

Transparent Glue Questions (People)

1. How have you used technology to cheat a system?

2. Has technology ever hurt you?

CHAPTER 17 – MONEY QUESTIONS

Money. Most are never satisfied with what they have and the wealthiest never sit back and say, "We have enough." Money causes feuds with families, spouses, and friends. Yet there are some that are wise money managers. Some have a strong plan on how they will retire debt free. Regardless of your situation, these questions are fun to debate in the employee break room over a peanut butter sandwich.

White Glue Questions (Money)

1. How much do you spend on hair and/or nails each month?

2. If you won a million dollars, what would you do with it?

3. If you won a billion dollar lottery, what is the very first thing you would purchase?

4. In what month did you file your tax return this year?

5. What was the highest grocery bill you ever had?

6. What one store would you like to win a shopping spree for?

7. Are you are early tax preparer or do you wait until the last minute?

8. Have you ever won an office pool?

9. If you went an electronics store right now with $1000, what would you buy?

10. About how much money do you usually spend on lunch each day?

11. When you retire, how will you spend all the money you invested?

12. Is it easier to give monetarily or with your time?

13. What is the best way to purchase a new car?

14. What is one thing you do each day that you would pay someone else to do?

15. When and what was the first purchase you made on Amazon.com (or pick some other site)?

16. If you were to be given a $1000 gift card from any store, what physical place of business would you pick?

17. Have you ever wanted to "downsize" your home or automobile due to a financial situation?

18. How much do you spend on groceries each week/month?

19. How much do you spend on eating out (restaurants) each week/month?

Yellow Glue Questions (Money)

1. If you won a million dollars and had to donate 50 percent to a charity, which would you pick?

2. When you retire, will you live off of what you saved or what someone saved for you?

3. What is the most expensive thing you wished you never bought?

4. Would you ever loan a significant amount of money to a friend/relative?

5. What store shows up the most on your monthly credit card bill?

6. Besides Amazon.com, what website do you purchase the most items?

Transparent Glue Questions (Money)

1. Do you think you have enough money for retirement?

2. Are you relying on an inheritance for a future need?

3. Who spends the most money within this team/group/family?

4. How much should each one of us give back?

5. If you had to spend five percent of your income each day,

   what would you do?

CHAPTER 18 – BOOKS & MUSIC QUESTIONS

Are you part of a "Book Club?" These are great questions to kick-start your meeting before you dive into the details of your literature. They can also save you when the one-hour book club meeting runs dry on discussion topics with 25 minutes to go.

Do you tend to be a lover of music? As with many topics, music is so diverse and can lead to many interesting findings. You might have a close friend who rocks out to 80s hairbands or that real quiet girl who works on your team has a local bluegrass band that she travels with on weekends. Regardless of your book or music tastes, write down some of these answers as it may turn you to something completely new and exciting to explore.

White Glue Questions (Books/Music)

1. If you could have written any book, what book would you like to have written?

2. What was the title of the last self-help book you read and did it help?

3. What is the longest book you have ever read?

4. If you were on a deserted island, what two books would you want with you?

5. What was your favorite book growing up?

6. What one book do you always associate it with school because you were forced to read in for a class?

7. What is your favorite part of the newspaper?

8. What is the last book you read?

9. How many books have you read this year?

10. How many magazines have you read from front to back this year?

11. Do you wake up to a specific song/band, the radio, or an alarm?

12. If you had a "theme song" that played whenever you walk into a room full of people, what would you want it to be?

13. What is your favorite song to sing in the car or shower?

14. If you had one song to play at your wedding what would it be?

15. Name a favorite sound, past or present.

16. Who was your favorite band, group, or solo artist when you were in high school?

17. What album would your friends be surprised that you own?

18. What musical instrument have you always aspired to play?

19. What song reminds you most of the disco era?

20. What song would you sing for the finale of American Idol (or any other singing completion)?

21. Who is the worst musician or musical group?

22. On a scale from 1 to 10 (10 highest), how well do you sing in the shower?

23. If you could see any musician, live or dead, perform their final concert, who would you choose?

24. What was the most memorable (good or bad) concert you have attended?

25. What was the song that was constantly playing during your favorite summer year.

26. How often do you change out the music you listen to either in the car, at work, or the gym?

27. What device did you use as a child to listen to music?

28. What song does everyone sing the wrong lyrics?

Yellow Glue Questions (Books/Music)

1. If you were to write a book what would it be about?

2. If you were stranded on a desert island, what book would you pick to read out loud each day to the other survivors?

3. If you wrote a book about yourself, what theme would it be about?

4. What book has influenced you greatly and why?

5. What album/CD/song is in the one you listen to the most this week?

6. Name the song title that best describes your life.

7. What's the best sound effect you can make and can you demo it for us now?

Transparent Glue Questions (Books/Music)

1. What do you read that elevates your life?

2. What do you listen to that elevates your perspectives on life?

3. Have you ever written your own music and can you share some of that with the group?

4. What book do you recommend to others that has drastically changed your life?

5. Has there ever been a time when music took you to a very dark place?

CHAPTER 19 – THE GROUP QUESTIONS

If you want to change your team's focus from external to internal, this is the section for your group. These questions may stretch your team beyond their comfort zone and can even open up the groups opinion of you. These questions can be a catalyst for team bonding but just as quickly can cause strife and hurt feelings. Know your team well before jumping into some of these tough questions.

White Glue Questions (Groups)

1. List 10 items everyone in the group has in common.

2. How would a dictionary define the person on your right?

3. Say one nice compliment about someone in this room.

4. If you could only take three people to an island in this group, whom would you pick and why?

5. On a scale from one to ten (ten the highest), how funny is the person to your left?

6. What is the nicest quality of the person on your right?

7. What game show would you recommend the person on your left should be a contestant because they would do very well?

8. Look at the person to your right...if you could pick an ice cream flavor to represent them, what would it be and why?

9. What are the greatest strengths of this team?

10. Show the last three pictures on your phone and give a reason why you took them.

11. Who in this group would you want to team up with to answer trivia questions about pop culture?

12. Who in this group would you want to team up with to answer trivia questions about world history?

13. Who in this group would get along best with your family and why?

14. Who in our group would be willing to eat a bowl of worms for $50,000?

15. What is the one work event you missed that is constantly talked about in this group?

16. If you could paint this office any color, what would you choose?

17. As a group, where would we agree on to live—by the ocean, in the mountains, or in the woods?

18. What animal would you adopt as the group pet?

19. Who in the group logs the most working hours?

20. Who in the group has the messiest office or desk?

21. If you were in charge of catering a meal for this group, what would you get?

22. What meeting causes the most conflict on this team?

23. What would you miss the most from this group/team/office if you could only be a part of the group remotely (not present)?

Yellow Glue Questions (Groups)

1. Ask the person to the right a question that you have always wanted to know about them.

2. Who in your group/team/office need an anger management refresher?

3. What did you do today to bring your team/group closer or make them a tighter knit group?

4. What one area of our team's performance would we want to improve the most?

5. What area on the team needs the most attention?

6. What word does the person to your right always use?

7. What does the person to your left do to waste time at work?

8. Create a nickname for the person to your left.

9. What story about this group gets shared the most?

10. If you needed someone to work with your most difficult customer, neighbor, or other coworker—whom would you pick from our team?

Transparent Glue Questions (Groups)

1. If this were your last day alive, what would you say to each person in the group?

2. If this were the last day of being a part of this group, what would you say to each person in the group?

3. What is this group most proud of and why?

4. Who in this group is (or will be) the most successful?

5. Name the one person on this team that you want to be more like.

CHAPTER 20 – WEIRD & RANDOM QUESTIONS

Do you have a drawer in your kitchen that has all of the random things you have found in your house? Let me guess the contents:

- Keys from a car you owned and sold five years ago

- A charger to a phone from over 10 years ago

- Five pens that do not work

- A screw that looks important, so you cannot throw it away

Sound familiar? So the questions in this chapter are my "junk drawer" questions. They really do not have a home in any other chapter, and for being so random (and sometimes silly!) they are really interesting questions to ask your group. It's the one chapter I debated back and forth if I should keep it in or out, but sometimes it's just fun to be silly. Kids and young adults will flock to these questions, so be prepared to answer these questions on a long car ride to grandma's house.

White Glue Questions (Weird/Random)

1. If you won a yacht, what would you name it?

2. If you were a Smurf, what would your name be?

3. What cartoon character best represents your personal philosophy?

4. Which of Snow White's seven dwarfs describes you best and why? (Doc, Happy, Bashful, Sleepy, Sneezy, Grumpy, Dopey)

5. If you were a professional wrestler, what would your ring name be and why?

6. If you had to describe your day as a traffic sign, what would it be?

7. If you were a spy what would your alias be?

8. If you could be a cartoon film character, who would you be?

9. If you were a pirate, what would your name be?

10. If you were a piece of fruit, what fruit would you choose to be?

11. If you were a tree, what kind of tree would you be and why?

12. What is the cutest animal on Earth?

13. What animal do you most enjoy seeing at the zoo?

14. Name a favorite sound, past or present.

15. If there were a whole different concept of reality (similar to the movie "The Matrix") what would it be?

16. If you were the eighth dwarf from Snow White, what would your name be?

17. If you could be any superhero, which one would you be and why?

18. What's your favorite fabric and why?

19. If someone gave you an island what would you name it and what would you do with it?

20. If you were a super hero what would your special power be and why did you pick that one?

21. If you could have a condiment dispensed from your navel, what would it be?

22. If you could be invisible for one day, where would you like to go?

23. If you could mix three animals together, which ones would you choose to make the ultimate animal?

24. When did you last climb a tree?

25. If you could be one Disney character whom would you be and why?

26. If you owned a pet monkey, what is the one trick you would want it to do?

27. What is the most disturbing sound in the world?

28. What is the biggest advantage of being small?

29. What is the most disgusting smell in the world?

30. If you could cause the extinction of any three creatures, what three would you choose?

31. Whose mind, besides your own, would you like to control?

32. What one person or thing best represents the 1990s?

33. What one person or thing best represents the 1980s?

34. What one person or thing best represents the 1970s?

35. If you were scuba diving, what underwater creature would scare you the most?

36. Name two things that you consider a "passing fad."

37. What is the best "gag gift" you have ever received?

38. What was your favorite decade? (50s, 60s, 70s, 80s, etc.)

39. What is a famous number?

40. What is your most favorite pair of shoes ever worn?

41. Describe your favorite pair of pajamas and how long have you had them?

42. How many handbags do you own?

43. What's the oldest piece of clothing you still own and wear?

44. When have you gone against a fashion trend?

45. How many pairs of jeans do you own?

46. What store is most represented in your wardrobe?

47. What is your favorite piece of clothing you own?

48. Describe your favorite type of house?

49. What do you do when you're at home?

50. What is your favorite house decor style? (Traditional, Contemporary, Country, Colonial, etc.)

51. Name all the kinds of trees in your yard right now.

52. When you lose electricity/power in a storm, do you light candles or turn on a flashlight and how many of each do you own?

53. If you didn't live in the city where you're living now, what city would you choose to be living in?

54. If you were to add one room to your house, what would it be?

55. What is the biggest inconvenience about the place you are currently living in?

56. What's the kindest act you have ever seen done (either to/by you or another)?

57. If you were a police officer, what type of criminal would you most want behind bars?

58. What world changing event would you like to take credit for?

59. What is the worst possible name to call a child?

60. If you were elected mayor of your city, what would be your first improvement, and why?

61. If you could serve as vice president under any past president in US history, with the knowledge you have today, whom would you choose?

62. If you had to endure one natural disaster (i.e. hurricane, tornado, etc), what would you pick and why?

63. What is your favorite winter activity?

64. What do you think is the most enjoyable thing to do in the snow?

65. What oceanic creature fascinates you?

Yellow Glue Questions (Weird/Random)

1. Why do you (or don't you) vote?

2. If you were city commissioner of (your home town), what would you do to make the city better?

3. If you could, would you want to become the President of the United States?

4. If you were in the "Miss America" talent competition, what would your talent be? (Note: both guys & gals have to answer this question!)

5. If you were forced to get a piercing on your body, which part of your body would you choose?

6. What's the most interesting "Ice Breaker" question you have ever been asked?

7. If someone rented a billboard for you, what would you put on it and where would it be located?

8. Besides a cat or dog, what animal would you want as a house pet?

9. What incentive would stop you from EVER driving drunk?

10. What incentive would stop you from EVER eating a donut again?

11. Describe the most inappropriate present that you received.

12. Have you ever seen a case where superiority gets mistaken for excellence?

13. What are some things that were repugnant, but now are found acceptable?

14. If you could be permanently one color for the rest of your life, what color would you choose and why?

15. What is the worst physical handicap that you would struggle with the most?

16. If you could rid the world of one thing, what would it be?

17. What do you consider the greatest threat to mankind?

18. Who do you think your country will fight its next war against?

19. If you could ask the president of your country one question, what would it be?

20. What protest march might somebody spot you at?

21. If one unsolved mystery could be solved in your lifetime, what would you choose?

22. If you had unlimited money and space, what one thing would you add to your kitchen?

23. What is your greatest environmental concern?

24. If you could rid the world of one thing, what would it be?

Transparent Glue Questions (Weird/Random)

1. What is your biggest frustration with your government?

2. What's something that made you so angry, but when you think about it now, it's really something silly?

3. Select one of the following that you want more in your life, but in order to get it, you need to select another that you will get less of: Love, Trust, Laughter, Patience, Peace, Family, Deep Conversations.

4. When was the last time you told someone honestly how you felt, not knowing if they were going to cry or laugh?

5. Are you considered old fashioned by any of your family or close friends?

6. What animal have you saved or feel should be treated as an endangered species?

7. What is the greatest mystery to you?

8. Could you ever vote for another political party and have you done that in the past?

9. Name one thing that is too serious to be joked about.

10. What current event do you find morally outrageous?

CHAPTER 21 – TAKING IT DEEPER

Questions, just like people, come in all shapes and sizes. There are big questions, trivial questions, brilliant questions, foolish questions, multiple-choice questions, and questions without answers. But knowing what to ask can be as important as recognizing the answer.

If you want to take the question and answer session to the next level, you must start off with learning how to listen. There are countless numbers of great books that dive into the topic of listening, but let me give you five quick tips that I have found to increase my own listening skills.

1. Close your computer (laptop) or turn off the sound on all of your devices when asking questions. Popups from email or

that little "ding" will immediately draw your attention away

from the speaker. This also includes your cell phone.

Nothing screams "you are not important" more than when

you are answering a question and the recipient of your

answer is eyeballing his mobile phone screen.

2. Choose your best time. Are you a better listener in the

morning or afternoon? Find your sweet spot for listening

and schedule those important discussions in that

timeframe.

3. Look at the speaker. That sounds simple and almost too

easy, but when someone is talking to you and you are

darting your eyes to items around the room, it limits your

ability to give 100 percent to the conversation.

4. Stop thinking about YOUR response. How many times do

you hear something and then form your answer and wait

for a pause to speak your opinion? What is your guess to how much you listened during the tail end of that discussion?

5. Ask the best (and simplest) follow-up question:

Tell me more.

That question gives the speaker PERMISSION to tell the entire story; not just the quick version that they have to squeeze into everyone else's attention span. You may hear more of the emotion...more of the inner thoughts...and it might even be the first time the speaker has discussed this topic out loud to this depth.

Follow these five simple steps and your discussions have the potential to get much deeper.

APPENDIX A – AUTHORS TOP 11 FAVORITE QUESTIONS TO ASK

I've been asking questions for years and of all the questions in this book, the ones below tend to be my "go-to" questions when I am in a new group session. There are so many to choose from and it really boils down to the situation and the people involved. If I was forced to pick my favorite 11, here are the questions that drove outstanding conversations and stories within my groups. So sit back and enjoy the group discussion!

1. What was your high and low for the day? (Chapter 4)

2. What was your favorite childhood toy? (Chapter 5)

3. How many places have you lived? Share the number of physical residences and/or the number of cities. (Chapter 5)

4. What was your favorite TV show when you were growing up? (Chapter 6)

5. What's the hardest thing you've ever done? (Chapter 7)

6. What is your favorite restaurant and why? (Chapter 8)

7. What is the most memorable vacation you had as a child? (Chapter 9)

8. If you could go back and change your career path, what would you be doing now? (Chapter 13)

9. What is the last book you read? (Chapter 18)

10. On a scale from one to ten (ten the highest), how funny is the person to your right? (Chapter 7)

11. What's the best sound effect you can make and can you demo it for us now? (Chapter 18)

APPENDIX B – YOUR TOP 20 QUESTIONS

Questions are only good if you can remember to ask them! Use

this page to capture your favorite questions.

QUESTION / PAGE

1. _____ / _____

2. _____ / _____

3. _____ / _____

4. _____ / _____

5. _____ / _____

6. _____ / _____

7. _____ / _____

8. _____ / _____

9. _____ / _____

QUESTION / PAGE

10. _____ / _____

11. _____ / _____

12. _____ / _____

13. _____ / _____

14. _____ / _____

15. _____ / _____

16. _____ / _____

17. _____ / _____

18. _____ / _____

19. _____ / _____

20. _____ / _____

ACKNOWLEDGEMENT

These questions never started out as a "book concept," but the book came to fruition by numerous people encouraging me to share this idea (and my questions) with others.

For the very first group that heard my question—thank you for allowing me to experiment on you! You grumbled and complained about a "Daily Traction Meeting," but in a short time it became a valuable part of your day. We shared many laughs, a couple tears, and bonded like no other team could bond. The questions I asked did not make us into a great team—it was the shared experience of the answers that brought us together. Thank you to Kirk Collins, Dawn Collins, Larry Karraker, Drew Norris, Jon Delaney, Kenny Meyer, Sherelyn Roberson, Steve Rediger, Tim Roberts, Kerry Wenzel, Russ Shirley, and Alisa Mueller.

I also want to thank the folks who got added to the original team—and proved out the theory that new people became acclimated quickly by answering the daily question. Some of these newbies included: Cory Venable, Michael Brown, Luke Florell, Mark Norris, Mike Jackson, and Mark McCauley.

For my newest team at VersionOne—thanks for letting me test out new questions on you! We have laughed way too much, but even more, have shared childhood stories that I will remember for a lifetime. Thank you Josiah Bernard, John (Solo) Boghos, Mark Irvin, Carlena Morris, Donnie (Dominic) Nix, and Avi Sistla.

The greatest question ever—this question did not become the greatest until it was experienced with all of these folks who traveled with me over the last six years on a Missions Trip to Macedonia to work with some great kids at an orphanage. This question brought so many laughs along with many tears—and ended up being the highlight for so many of my trips. A deep thanks to all of you for donating your time to this great cause:

Steve (Stevo) Shugart, Dan Daube, Melody Mitchell, Carol Stampley, Elizabeth Burton, Kellie Reich, Gary & Susan Coryell, Caroline Joiner, Teresa Cook, Nathan & Mary Cox, Jill Wood, Mark & Jennifer Fisher, Kristina Donald, Brenda Daube, Rebecca Johnson, Todd Stevens, Dustin Kawa, Greta (Gretchen) Smith, John & Haley Lenker, Nancy Ford, Amy Gill, Victoria Link, Casey Holloway, James Payne, Stephanie Norris, Dawn Evans, and Cathie Gober.

Dustin Kawa – thanks for dreaming up the first book cover idea back in 2014. It was just a sketch, but it motivated me to continue with this crazy idea.

Special thanks to Cory Wheeler—your continual questions about this book have kept me motivated to cross the finish line.

Special thanks to my editing crew: Sandra Rohren, Teresa Towey, Elizabet Makedonia, and a plethora of others behind the scenes making this the best possible reflection of the Group Glue concept. Reading through all of the concepts, then rough drafts riddled with flaws and errors that eventually became this finished product with you keen eye for details.

Shout out to one great company—VersionOne! The culture there needs its own book written. Thanks to Robert and Ian for your continued support of my daily questions...and your crazy answers! Holly—you may have answered more questions than anyone on the board—thanks!

Many of my questions were "tested" out on a church small group I led with my wife. Their reactions to these questions helped me decide what questions would really drive discussions within a group. We have laughed, we have shed tears, but in the end it was just fun sharing life with these folks. Thanks to all of those folks for encouraging me to come up with more questions!

Great big thank you to two amazing people—Brad & Jiyoung Bretz. You invited us into your small group many years ago and have always been supportive and encouraging to my entire family.

Family comes first, but I wanted to end my acknowledgement with them—because you were the supporting foundation and encouragement that kept me writing. Without the love and support of my wife Teresa and son's Tyler, Braden and Carson, this book may very well have ended up as just an idea stuck on a list in EverNote.com.

ABOUT THE AUTHOR

Jeff Cook is a business leader residing in Atlanta, GA with a knack for coming up with questions from the most random subjects. This book was an inspiration from many years of asking questions to the various "groups" he was a part of whether at work, church, volunteering or with friends.

This book covers what Jeff discovered over years of asking questions to his numerous teams. The question—asked in a group setting—created an opportunity for the group to experience the answer of a teammate. Those shared stories, over time, led to a team that bonded like GLUE. Continued "question experiences" led to improved team cohesiveness, deeper understanding of their teammate, and a bonding shared over similar experiences.

REAL QUOTES

When writing a book, many famous authors get their famous friends to slap a nice quote on the front or back and it adds some validity to book. I had thought about asking some of my own celebrity friends, but soon realized I don't have any! So I just asked those that have been exposed to my questions to tell me how it impacted them. These are normal folks like you and me, so my hope is that you are impacted as much as they were.

The quotes are unedited (except for a few grammar mistakes) and tell you the honest truth about how these questions and this book have made an impact on them. Here are some of my favorites.

"Jeff Cook's book Group Glue has opened the gateway to meaningful conversations with my children, family and friends. His questions have given me the confidence to speak with new people I meet and individuals at networking events. This book is a continual resource for me in my personal and professional life."

- Amy Rose Gill

"As we get older, our memories and experiences begin to hide behind the layers of our current existence and activities. We live in a busy world of work, family commitments, bills and more bills. In the process of growing old and dealing with our present lives, many of us repress an important part of ourselves. Our lives' routine represses our youth and the simple things that gave us joy. We almost completely forget the details of a time when we were innocent and content, a time when we were unknowingly building who we are going to be. Our first kiss, our favorite cereal and our first plane ride, all act as distinct markers in our lives. These objects and events seeded our expectations, our desires and began to build the path to our futures. When Jeff presented the questions to our group, we didn't understand that the questions would help us uncover some of our repressed past. Those questions were like tools in the hands of a skilled archaeologist, gently digging up forgotten artifacts, slowly brushing away the erosion and debris from the daily grind all to reveal some of the golden pieces of who we are."

-Mark Irvin

"I remember years ago the first time Jeff asked me what my HI/LO was for the day. I was part of a missions team in an Eastern Europe country called Macedonia. I thought to myself "What?" I never, ever asked myself that question before. Once I began to think about my answer, I relived my *whole* day, the big AND little parts. It gave me a different and new perspective on what actually transpired during that one, single day. Sometimes a *little* part would be my Hi or Lo for the day and that little part effected the *entire day* in a certain way. The HI/LO question is an incredible way to understand people in group setting by seeing through their eyes a different perspective of the day and how it affected them. Sometimes it's the same perspective as mine, other times opposite, or not at all what I would expect! Regardless, the HI/LO question helps me personally to see things more in detail and also assists me to understand *more* how others perceive the same experiences. The HI/LO question helps me grow as an individual with each day and helps my relationships grow with others in a group setting. "

- Elizabeth Burton

"Jeff introduced me to his bombardment of questioning a few years ago in front of a group of complete strangers, sitting in a room together, preparing to spending the next ten days with each other traveling overseas on a mission trip. Honestly, that first date type awkwardness filled the room. Jeff opened that first meeting with a simple question, and we all began to sit there anxiously waiting for our turn to share. With every answer given we were learning so much about the people whom were complete strangers only moments before. It's amazing how one simple question can tear down walls, build stronger teams, inspiring countless hours of conversations, and even create long lasting friendships. Thanks Jeff."

- Todd Richard Stevens

HAVE A QUESTION?

Ask.

Jeff@GroupGlueBook.com

Made in United States
North Haven, CT
17 March 2022

17251103R00127

What do you hate spending money on? Hopefully not books with over 1000 questions designed to bring your team, tribe, or group closer together. Through years of asking questions to his own teams, author Jeffrey T. Cook discovered that questions—asked in a group setting—create an opportunity for the group to experience the answer of a teammate. Those shared stories, over time, lead to teams that bond like GLUE. Continued "question experiences" result in improved team cohesiveness, deeper understanding of their teammates, and a bonding shared over similar experiences.

Using GLUE as a metaphor, these questions are categorized in levels from very basic (What was your favorite childhood toy?) to very deep (Are there any relatives or siblings you no longer talk to?). ASK THE QUESTION AND EXPERIENCE THE ANSWER!

JEFFREY T. COOK has been leading teams for nearly two decades. His use of questions has created a binding of his teams that lead to more authentic relationships. This book was an inspiration from many years of asking questions to the various "groups" he was a part of whether at work, church, volunteering or with friends. Born and raised in the Midwest, he now resides in Atlanta, GA with his wife and three boys. To this day, their family dinner conversation revolves around the "best question ever asked".

ISBN 9780998126616

9 780998 126616

90000

www.GroupGlueBook.com